STARS OF HIP-HOP

KANYE WEST

RAP SUPERSTAR AND FASHION DESIGNER

TOM HEAD AND
DEIRDRE HEAD

Enslow Publishing

101 W. 23rd Street
Suite 240
New York, NY 10011
USA

enslow.com

Published in 2020 by Enslow Publishing, LLC.
101 W. 23rd Street, Suite 240, New York, NY 10011

Library of Congress Cataloging-in-Publication Data

Names: Head, Tom, author. | Head, Deirdre, author.
Title: Kanye West : rap superstar and fashion designer / Tom Head and Deirdre Head.
Description: New York : Enslow Publishing, 2020. | Series: Stars of hip-hop |
Audience: 2 | Includes bibliographical references and index.
Identifiers: LCCN 2018051110| ISBN 9781978509627 (library bound) | ISBN
9781978510227 (pbk.) | ISBN 9781978510241 (6 pack)
Subjects: LCSH: West, Kanye—Juvenile literature. | Rap musicians—United States—
Biography—Juvenile literature.
Classification: LCC ML3930.W42 H43 2020 | DDC 782.421649092 [B] —dc23
LC record available at https://lccn.loc.gov/2018051110

Printed in the United States of America

To Our Readers: We have done our best to make sure all websites in this book were
active and appropriate when we went to press. However, the author and the publisher
have no control over and assume no liability for the material available on those
websites or on any websites they may link to. Any comments or suggestions can be
sent by email to customerservice@enslow.com.

CONTENTS

FROM GEORGIA TO CHINA

Kanye West is a superstar. He always knew he wanted to be great at whatever he did.

Kanye Omari West was born on July 8, 1977, in Atlanta, Georgia. His mother was named Donda. She grew up in Oklahoma. Donda earned her PhD degree. She taught people how to speak English. She also taught college courses. Kanye's father was named Ray. Ray grew up in a military family. He took pictures for a newspaper.

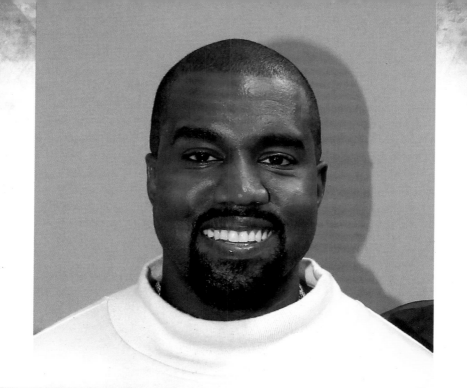

Kanye West smiles during a fashion show in Paris, France. He has found success in music and fashion.

Ray and Donda taught Kanye to work hard. They also taught him to believe in himself. He was their only child. Kanye's parents wanted him to do great things.

Donda wrote a book called *Raising Kanye* in 2007. She talked about his childhood and what it was like being his mom.

LIFE IN CHICAGO

Donda and Ray divorced when Kanye was three years old. Donda took Kanye and moved from Georgia to Chicago. She began a job as an English professor at Chicago State University. Kanye visited his father every summer.

Donda read history books to Kanye at night. She raised him to love learning. Ray taught Kanye to think for himself.

Early Talent

In preschool, Kanye was very good at drawing pictures. His teachers noticed this right away. He didn't just draw stick figures. He drew detailed pictures of people.

Together they taught him to trust his own mind. It worked. Kanye was a talented artist even as a child. He also had strong opinions. His mother said, "He's never wanted to do anything halfway."[1]

Kanye West stands with his mother, Donda West, in 2007.

Young Kanye felt like an outsider in China.
Not many black people lived there.

A YEAR IN CHINA

Kanye was ten years old in 1987.
That year, Donda was asked to teach
at Nanjing University. This school is
in China. She said yes and brought
Kanye with her. Donda taught English

to Chinese young adults. Kanye quickly learned how different China was from the United States.

Kanye learned **Mandarin Chinese**. But he didn't fit in. His classmates had never seen a black person before. They kept touching his hair and skin. His mother took him out of school. She taught him at home. They spent a year in China. Then they came back to the United States.

"I think being in China got me ready to be a celeb because, at that time, a lot of Chinese [people] had never seen a black person."[2]

GROWING UP IN CHICAGO

2

Donda and Kanye went back to Chicago in 1988. Donda returned to her job at Chicago State University. She could come home as soon as Kanye left school. Sometimes she brought him to work with her.

Kanye joined a dance group. He practiced his dance moves in the mirror. He also entered talent shows. He loved helping

Kanye performs at a 2009 concert. He was certain of his talent from an early age.

other contestants. But he wouldn't let them help him. He thought he was too good to need anyone else's help.

STATE OF MIND

Kanye and his friends grew up in the 1980s. They loved listening to the music of the time. Kanye especially loved the hip-hop bands Kid 'n Play and De La Soul. Soon Kanye and his friends wanted to record their own music.

At thirteen, Kanye and two of his friends formed a band. They called themselves State of Mind. They rented a basement **studio** for $25 an hour.[1] They practiced

A Dr. Seuss Song

The song Kanye recorded with his friends was called "Green Eggs and Ham." The title came from the Dr. Seuss book of the same name.

and recorded a song. It was Kanye's first experience as a musician. He loved it. But he focused more on his music than on his studies. His grades started slipping.

Kid 'n Play was one of Kanye's favorite groups.

ACTING UP

Kanye West always knew he had talent. He always believed he would be a superstar. He always thought he would change the world. Some people thought he was full of himself. It sometimes made him hard to deal with.

"People always tell you, 'Be humble. Be humble.' When was the last time someone told you to be amazing? Be great! Be great! Be awesome! Be awesome!"[2]

Many young people struggle with being selfish. Kanye did, too. He was full of creative ideas. Sometimes it was hard for him to realize other people also had creative ideas. He thought he was going to get a record deal when

Kanye worked on other people's music
before he made it as a rapper.

he was thirteen. He didn't realize how hard
it would be.

His mother, Donda, noticed Kanye began
misbehaving at home. She told him she
didn't like how he was acting. He promised
he would do better.

MUSIC PRODUCER

Kanye has a cousin named Tony Williams. Williams noticed Kanye's talent. He taught Kanye how to use drum machines and **sample** music. He also helped Kanye meet people who worked in the music business. One of them was a DJ named No I.D. No I.D. helped Kanye learn more about making music.

Kanye worked hard to raise money to buy studio **equipment**. His mother helped him get started.

Kanye also showed an early interest in fashion. Donda would give him money to buy clothes. But he didn't spend it on a closet full of cheap clothes. Instead he

No I.D. gives a speech in 2017. He taught Kanye about music when Kanye was just getting started.

bought a few expensive pieces. He wore them over and over.

THE HIGH SCHOOL YEARS

Kanye was a gifted student when he was young. But his grades went down as he got

Kanye receives his honorary PhD on May 11, 2015.

older. He was more interested in music than he was in his classes. His mother worried he might not graduate.

Kanye refused to choose between schoolwork and his music career. He wanted to become successful at both. And he was. Kanye graduated from high school on time.

DOWN TO BUSINESS

West started at the American Academy of Art in Chicago for painting. Then he

An Honor

In 2015, Kanye West received an **honorary** PhD from the School of the Art Institute in Chicago. Earlier that year, he said he would have gone there "if [he] could have done it again."[1]

changed schools and **majors**. He studied English at Chicago State University.

A local **producer** named Grav noticed West's talent. He began to pay him thousands of dollars for his work. Then West produced Grav's first album in 1996. It was called *Down to Earth*. It was very popular in Chicago. It made both Grav and West famous in the hip-hop scene.

"I try to get as close to a childlike level as possible because we were all artists back then."[2]

Down to Earth proved West could be a successful producer. Word spread of his talent. But West could not study and produce music at the same time. He decided to

Kanye poses for a photograph with Jay-Z in 2004.

drop out of college to focus on his career. He started producing work for rising artists. Soon he was working with Jay-Z, Beyoncé, and Ludacris.

BECOMING A SUPERSTAR

By 2002, West was already a successful producer. But he wanted to release his own music. He was working on his debut album, *The College Dropout*. Then something terrible happened. He was in a bad car accident that October. He broke his jaw. It could have ended his career. Instead it made him famous. He recorded "Through the Wire" in the hospital. He

Kanye holds his first three Grammy trophies.

rapped while his jaw was still wired shut. It became the first of many hits.

West won his first Grammy Award in 2005. He won Best Rap Album for *The*

College Dropout. He also won Best Rap Song for "Jesus Walks."

West also became a fashion **icon**. He made **shutter shades** popular. He designed sneakers for Nike and Adidas.

Kanye West and his wife, Kim Kardashian West, attend a 2014 museum event.

LOVE AND LOSS

In 2014, West married celebrity Kim Kardashian. They have three children.

His music and fashion designs have earned him a fortune. He has released eleven hit albums. His life seems perfect. But one of the most important people is missing from his life.

"As my grandfather would say, 'Life is a performance.' I'm giving all that I have in this life."[1]

West's mother, Donda, died on November 10, 2007. She died a day after having **plastic surgery**. He blamed himself for her death. "If I had never moved to [Los Angeles]," he said, "she'd be alive."[2] He often talks about her in his music.

KANYE'S TALENT IS RECOGNIZED

Kanye West has won twenty-one Grammy Awards. This is the same number as Jay-Z. So far, no rapper has won more Grammys than either of them. West has also won many other music awards.

He has also become a famous fashion designer. His sneakers won a Shoe of the Year Award in 2015. His clothing lines draw large crowds at fashion shows all over the world.

Giving Back

West has used his fame to help others. He started a music program in Chicago. He also helped raise millions for people hurt by Hurricane Katrina in 2005.

Kanye wears his famous shutter shades at the 2007 MTV Video Music Awards. He continues to make a splash in music and fashion.

In 2016, *USA Today* put out an article called "Is Kanye West the Greatest Artist of the 21st Century?" Many think so.

Kanye West's childhood dreams have come true. He became great at what he does.

TIMELINE

1977 Kanye West is born in Atlanta, Georgia, on June 8.

1996 West begins writing and producing for Chicago rapper Grav's *Down to Earth* album, beginning his long career as a music producer.

2002 On October 2, West is injured in a bad car accident. He records "Through the Wire" while his jaw is still wired shut. It becomes his first radio single.

2004 West releases his debut album, *The College Dropout*.

2005 West wins his first three Grammy Awards, including Best Rap Album for *The College Dropout* and Best Rap Song for "Jesus Walks."

2007 On November 10, West's mother, Donda, dies after surgery.

2009 Hoping to learn enough to become a designer himself, West takes on an internship at the Italian fashion company Fendi.

2012 West releases his first fashion collection.

2013 West's first child with Kim Kardashian, North, is born on June 15.

2014 West marries Kim Kardashian on May 24.

2015 West begins to release designer sneakers in collaboration with Adidas.

2015 His son, Saint, is born December 5.

2018 West begins offering his own line of designer homes.

2018 His daughter Chicago is born January 15.

CHAPTER NOTES

CHAPTER 1. FROM GEORGIA TO CHINA

1. Mark Beaumont, *Kanye West: God and Monster* (London, UK: Omnibus Press, 2015), book preview, accessed October 22, 2018, https://www.scribd.com/book/347337479/Kanye-West-God-Monster.

2. Chris Campion, "Classic Kanye West Interview: Breakdancing in China, Self Esteem Issues and the KKK," Sabotage Times, November 28, 2013, https://sabotagetimes.com/music/kanye-west-on-breakdancing-in-china-self-esteem-issues-and-the-kkk.

CHAPTER 2. GROWING UP IN CHICAGO

1. Karizza Sanchez, "The Most Stylish #KanyeMoments from His Mother Donda West's 2007 Book," Complex, May 10, 2015, https://www.complex.com/style/2015/05/best-style-moments-raising-kanye-donda-west-book/kanye-value-quality.

2. David Samuels, "American Mozart," *Atlantic,* May 2012, https://www.theatlantic.com/magazine/archive/2012/05/american-mozart/308931/?single_page=true.

CHAPTER 3. MUSIC PRODUCER

1. Zach Frydenlund, "Kanye West Spoke at Oxford University Earlier Today," Complex, March 2, 2015, https://www.

complex.com/music/2015/03/kanye-west-oxford-university-speech.

2. Steve McQueen, "Kanye West," *Interview,* January 14, 2014, https://www.interviewmagazine.com/music/kanye-west.

CHAPTER 4. BECOMING A SUPERSTAR

1. Steve McQueen, "Kanye West," *Interview,* January 14, 2014, https://www.interviewmagazine.com/music/kanye-west.

2. Madeline Boardman, "Kanye West Blames Himself for Mom Donda West's Death," *Us Weekly,* June 26, 2015, https://www.usmagazine.com/celebrity-news/news/kanye-west-blames-himself-for-mom-donda-wests-death-2015266/.

WORDS TO KNOW

equipment The machines and tools needed to do something.

honorary Given as a title to recognize success.

icon Someone people look up to.

major The subject a student studies in college.

Mandarin Chinese The most commonly spoken language in China.

plastic surgery Operations done to change how someone looks.

producer The person who is in charge of making, and sometimes providing the money for, a record.

sample To take a part of a song and use it for another song.

shutter shades Sunglasses that use horizontal strips of plastic instead of lenses.

studio A special room used to record music.

LEARN MORE

BOOKS

Burlingame, Jeff. *Kanye West: Hip-Hop Mogul*. Berkeley Heights, NJ: Speeding Star, 2014.

Hill, Laban Carrick. *When the Beat Was Born: DJ Kool Herc and the Creation of Hip Hop*. New York, NY: Roaring Brook Press, 2018.

Morse, Eric. *What Is Hip-Hop?* La Jolla, CA: Black Sheep, 2017.

WEBSITES

Billboard: Kanye West
www.billboard.com/music/kanye-west
Check out Kanye West's Billboard chart history, as well as videos and news.

Kanye West
kanyewest.com
Visit Kanye West's official site, with links to music videos, merchandise, and more.

INDEX